Run Therapy

A BITTER SWEET GUIDE TO RUNNING, EVOLUTION AND ICE CREAM

Publisher: Fixed Stars Enterprises, Dunsborough, Western Australia

First Published 2012

Title: Run Therapy www.facebook.com/RunTherapy

Author: Cohen, Andrew

Copyright © Andrew Cohen 2012

ISBN 978-0-646-58015-9

Layout & Design: Ink Box Graphics www.inkboxgraphics.com.au

Cover photo from 'The Longest Day' series by Christian Fletcher www.christianfletcher.com.au

May your feet carry you safely home.   The gate to the mountain is open.

From *The Epic of Gilgamesh* (c. 1800 BC)

WARNING: NON-SCIENCE CONTENT

This book is based on personal observations from an experiment with a sample size of approximately one. That would be me. I offer no scientifically valid proof. I don't claim to be objective. What follows is part opinionated rant, part unqualified speculation, part travelogue, part hope, part undisciplined abuse of adjectives and part a love song for my feet. Some of it is serious.

Even when it's not, I still think it's right.

Message from the Future

Dear Ancestors,

To those of you who ran and ate ice cream, thank you! It worked.

It's a beautiful world. ☺

Foreword

Conflict is strange. It's like wearing the wrong glasses - it changes our perception of everything.

Charlemagne's sword, *Joyeuse*, can be admired today, in oblique repose behind glass on the 1st floor of the Richelieu wing of the Louvre Museum in Paris, as an object of remarkable beauty and workmanship, glorifying the hand that held it. Believed by some to contain within its hilt splinters of the spear of Longinus, it is the undisputed emblem of an empire that re-lit the candle of elegant civilisation in Western Europe. By contrast, on the battlefield it was something less than noble, a herald of bloody death and impending taxes.

In a rather similar manner, the lasting virtues of running aren't seen in competition. Freed from the heartlessness of timing systems, the brutality of VO2max calculations, energy equations and femur length measurements, the angst of the taper and the fury of finishing lines, running takes us on a very different journey.

This book follows that other course, to a shout of joy and an irrepressible passion for nothing more than life itself. In the end, it's all we have, but it's also a whole lot more than we first think.

And when it's over, your finishing position will be of interest to no-one.

Glossary of Terms

Ice Cream

If there is a metaphor in this book, this is it. Ice cream stands for something that is at once both an uncomplicated, innocent, incorruptible pleasure and a justifiable, proportionate reward for effort. This might describe something other than ice cream – but I don't know what it is.

Running

Running is the outwardly simple act of putting your body in motion, and the less simple act of putting your mind at rest. It is unavoidably honest. To a runner, momentum is just a conspiracy of blackboard physicists, and when the will falters, so do the feet. Either you're running, or you've stopped.

6am Tuesday (Part 1)

This morning I saved a life.

My run stopped short where Tuesday's child lay stranded on the sand, abandoned by a low tide that, with ant-like precision, was turning too slowly. The dolphin sighed, and flapped with sad resignation. Clouds gathered in its eyes.

An hour later, eight people who had come together as strangers united to carry her, now bathed and beautiful, across the sand flats, back to the open sea. The ripples flashed in the early sun and the soft breeze carried news from far away, where blue meets blue, where dolphins live.

I ran home, barefoot through the rising shallows, and celebrated with an ice cream. Running always seems to take you to where good things happen.

On a morning tinged with grace running helped save a life.

As it always does.

Cryogenesis

The Future's in the Freezer

Neural Carbon

It is within us to change. The die has not been cast, nor is nature laughing at us.

No-one ever asks you why you walk. Walking has an implied reasonableness that running apparently hasn't. If you run, there will be questions. This has not always been the case. In times past, when food did not stand still in perfect, patterned rows on shelves, conveniently waiting to be caught, bought and eaten, running was an important life skill.

A lazy Darwinist might conclude from the mammoth-munching tribe of grunting hunter-gatherers camped around the base of our family tree that more gifted runners caught dinner, ate, and survived; bad runners starved, and their genetic material was reduced to dust on their bleached bones. More or less.

The problem with this is the implication that we are all prisoners of our DNA, and that some of us are born to die out. That really seems to make the whole process of fertilisation and gestation potentially amusing, but overall a bit futile. I prefer a different theory – that nature is mostly fair (or if not fair, then at least indifferent), and that the right to survive is not hard-wired at birth. It's what happens in our lifetime that echoes through the generations.

Suppose for a moment that our genetic ladder descends from those who tackled life head on, with the strength of will not just to chase down fast food, but to adapt and to persist until any challenge was beaten into submission. We're not all natural runners today, so it stands to reason that some of us got here by a different route.

The process of becoming a runner teaches perseverance, belief and acceptance. Running improves mental acuity, disease resistance and self-esteem. It also shows us that we're almost always capable of doing more than we think, and that we won't know exactly how much until we try.

The person who achieves and understands all this is well equipped to deal with life's hiccups, and deserves to survive, multiply and eat mountains of ice cream.

While, by accident of birth, one person may have the capacity to run faster than another, no-one has a natural advantage when it comes to making a commitment. The ability to commit is either encoded in freely available, common DNA, or it's part of some universal human spirit. Whatever the case, none of us is disqualified by nature from shaking the tree of life and taking its fruit. DNA is just AND backwards. In the sum of life it's a plus sign, not the total – not who we are, but who we can be. And we can always be more. If we fall short of our own potential, it wasn't predestined by a poor choice of parents. It's more likely something we learned, whether by circumstance or choice, and should, if given the chance, try to forget.

That might be easier said than done.

The modern world uses technology to move objects, bodies and ideas. That's all fine; however, this transfer of effort has a cost beyond the apparent threat of involuntary obesity. The first world human body might be inclining towards the spherical and horizontal, but the real risk is more than geometric: our will, individual and collective, is weakened and distracted by our faith in the seeming infallibility of databases and machine-made calculations.   We're becoming spectators to our own existence, learning not to take responsibility for who we are, what we know and who we will become.   Evolution's gentle sculpting is under siege by armies of 1s and 0s in impassive machines that are stealing our lives and reducing our need to work and to think. The near future probably won't be a dreary, dead-end dystopia of outsourced, silicon brains, exoskeletons and hackable, spam-filled memories, but it won't be wholly human either. It will be something less.

Which is rather sad.

It may well be that running is the best way to re-learn our potential, and to assert control over a balanced, carbohydrate burning, sweat and carbon-based future with hopes, dreams and passions that don't compute.

The Volume of a Cone

Seeming is the first step in a timeless transformation that leads to *becoming.* If ice cream makes our caterpillar world seem a better place, the world is more likely to become a butterfly.

Ice cream is much more than the sum of its calories.

When used responsibly as part of a sensible diet, ice cream represents most of what is good in life – it's free of pretence, it's uncomplicated, democratic and optimistic. In a world that tolerates molecular gastronomy and extreme cuisine, ice cream maintains a defiant humility. It's a fearless frontline soldier in the revolt of common sense against the disingenuous leadership, farce and excess of fashion.

Ice cream recalls good times. It elicits a smile. People consuming ice cream are rarely dangerous, vengeful or sad. They are not negative numbers in the sum of net global happiness. The ice cream eater is a friend, Friday's child, loving and giving. Time spent with ice cream is time spent not being naughty.

Running and ice cream make a great team - ice cream fuels a run, and a run earns an ice cream. Together they can lay the foundation for a better world: optimism built on honesty, ingenuity built on strength, community built on sustainability. A society committed to running and the guiltless consumption of ice cream would be a beautiful place to live. We may not get to see it, but we can model it. Then it will happen.

So, in one way, running – or more correctly, the process of becoming a runner - is really about building happiness, getting to eat all the ice cream you want and transforming the world, one caterpillar at a time, starting with yourself.

The Ascent

The journey from here to there

You're Here

There's no step tougher than the first – until the second. Starting out may be difficult, but keeping going is a truer test of character.

There's a fair chance you're reading this book because you're down at the bottom of a hole. You started running, but your motivation hit the wall. Or someone close to you thinks it's about to. You've had a glimpse of running in zero gravity, but couldn't fathom the aerodynamics. The machinery of good intent is frozen, or at least grinding inexorably to a halt.

Things looks grim, however this isn't the end. It's an opportunity to reconsider what's important. You can turn your back on the chance to change and stay where you are (you certainly won't lack company), or you can seize the opportunity and, like Huckleberry Finn, 'light out for the territory' any time you want, to where abundant adventures await. It's entirely your choice. Either way, the point is that almost anyone can reach the stage where running is natural, and where *not* running feels like something is missing. The question is not 'can you make it?', but 'do you want to?'

If you do, then you can.

Don't worry about whether or not you will win races: you'll do far better than that.

The journey from here to there is rather like trying to get lost. If you know where you're going, then you're not there yet. 'There' is where all paths meet and where the act of going doesn't imply a purpose or a destination. The beginning and end are the same place, no matter how far you travel.

You can think of it as a pilgrimage, if you like. It requires similar faith, but it's bound by a different covenant. Your destiny is in your own hands. No-one else will save you.

Falling Down

Running shoes should be clearly labelled: '*Motivation not included*'. They don't run on their own.

There are two roads leading to the hole you've fallen into. Whichever sorry trajectory applies to you, the crash site is the same.

Which path did you follow?

A. Few people start running with a clear goal. Generally they aren't running *to* anywhere – they're running *away*. Running looks like a simple, low-tech way to beat temptation. Sadly, most who try to fly are neither naturally ballistic nor buoyant at standard temperature and pressure, and they fail to reach escape velocity. Whatever they were fleeing is now so far behind that they've forgotten what it was; or they see the solution as worse than the problem. Either way, there seems no reason to continue. They shrug, plummet to earth on Icarus' broken wings, and go back to bed.

OR

B. The drive to compete is nearly irresistible. It's also almost always completely pointless. It's a losing game. Genetics isn't fair. If you're motivated by your relationship to time and distance, or if you constantly compare your performance to that of others, sooner or later you'll be defeated, disappointed and broken. The pain/gain ratio will resolve to an imaginary number. When that happens, you smash the alarm clock against the wall and go back to bed.

There's no hill steeper than a lack of motivation or the sense of clear and present failure. As the launch momentum stumbles, the whole world seems tilted, and running looks increasingly illogical. Bad voices in your head tell you to stop. You start to pay attention to advertisements for 'over 45 lifestyle villages' and finally work out how to use the digital TV remote control. More and more days begin with excuses.

So, now you're in bed, down a hole, rusted to the TV – and mostly because you missed the point of what running is all about. It's not pretty.

There are two roads in, but only one road out. This way, please.

The gate to the mountain is open.

Mind the step.

Getting Back Up

If life were a race, no-one would be in a rush to finish. If it's not a race, there's no rush either. However you solve the puzzle, the only meaningful goal is to get the most out of whatever life you have.

The path out of the hole starts with the acceptance that running and, eventually, ice cream are somehow linked to your personal salvation and your role as an agent of world happiness. This may initially sound silly, but there's no other way (and, in due course, it will soon make sense). The urge to outdo and the desire to escape have both failed miserably, leaving no-one happier, wiser, thinner or fitter.

What's required here is a new definition of running, a formulation centred on the individual rather than on some idealised average derived from absolute values like time and distance; one that leaves you with lasting fulfilment and the sweet taste of ice cream instead of the bitterness of unattained goals and the fading, inflated memory of past glories. If you can't accept that proposition, then this book probably ends here. Maybe there's something good on TV.

If, on the other hand, your aim is now true, and your passion is for more life rather than a terminal instant of triumph, the challenge is to sustain your motivation until you reach the point where it is no longer required: the self-perpetuating ice cream liberation threshold at the top of the hill. At that point, you can't not run, you can eat all the ice cream you want and you're an outstanding model for humanity. Way to go!

That's not to say it's all easy. On the way up, there will be difficult days when running is going to hurt - and there's nothing anywhere in any *User's Guide to Commitment* extolling the joys of masochism. That might look very much like the same problem that put you down the hole in the first place, but this time there's a critical difference.   The commitment required to complete this journey has a manageable, human scale – specifically, because we are no longer aiming to be better than anyone: we are trying to do exactly and only what each of us was individually designed to do.   Our success is already within us. It's just a trick of the light – no obstacle on the way is as big or as nasty as it appears from here.

To give yourself a better sense of the road ahead, take three small steps before you run.

First, recognise that competition of any sort is at best optional. Nowhere in the definition of running is there an obligation to compete. Racing is to running as sashimi is to fishing - an exotic variation which is not to everyone's taste and at which only a few excel. It's the unadorned, basic skill that provides the greatest satisfaction for the greatest number of people.

Running, as distinct from its functional variations, such as racing, chasing or fleeing, has no external goal or cause. It involves, for no reason other doing it, acting on an internally generated intent to engage the feet in an indefinite period of bipedal locomotion that expends more energy than walking. That intent, the willing it to happen, is at least half the journey – which explains why walking isn't a mid-point between being stationary and running: walking is either unconscious or the outcome of an entirely different exercise of the will. Two walks don't equal a run.

Second, set yourself a realistic and simple goal, one without the bureaucratic indifference of numbers. This should become an integral part of your brain's operating system, underpinning every open application. Download, install and run the following script:

'It's better to run more often than to run longer or faster.'

No matter how far or fast you run, or how much you improve, this rule will never change: frequency will always beat amplitude. The best measure of success is how often you start.

If that doesn't immediately make sense, you may need to re-boot and clear your running history.

And finally, commit only to those things you can control. You're trying to get past the wall, not bang your head against it. A laser does the bright things it does with remarkably little energy or effort largely because it's able to focus. The same principle applies to running. Your body already knows what running is (it's anything but unnatural); you only lack the confidence to do it because your mind is still wandering, sending you in the wrong direction or telling you to do too much. The right focus increases your chance of success, reduces the effort required to keep going and saves you a lot of headaches. Try these three low impact guidelines:

- *The only body you need to worry about is your own.* Treat training programs with suspicion – they're almost invariably right for someone who isn't you, for a day that isn't today or for a place that isn't here. Recognise your difference.

- *The only running rhythm that counts is your own.* When you race or run in a group, don't make a goal out of comparisons (to other runners or to your past). Run with others, but on your own terms. Be prepared to run alone.

- *The only thing you need to measure is your willingness to try.* The aim each day is to maintain the same level of perceived effort to overcome friction – both underfoot and in your head. How that effort translates to pace or distance is, on a day to day basis, completely, utterly and irrevocably irrelevant.

Your body, your rhythm, your perceived effort – these are all things you can control.

What you can't control is the timing of improvements in endurance and pace – so don't make any commitment to them. If you've got into the habit of running, they will happen when they are ready, and will be all the better for not having been rushed.

Practical tips

Ritual paves the road to a habit – and running is a habit you want, or need. As with any ritual, there are simple steps to follow to make it easier to get it right.

- Make friends with your shoes. Keep them in sight. Put them on and feel the sense of obligation to take them out somewhere. They know why they exist.

- Get used to starting on your own, regardless of the weather, when there is no-one and nothing except yourself to drag you out the door. Don't wait for a kick start.
- Let whatever happens, happen. Don't be pushed or pushy. Be patient. Days will be different, but don't think of them as better or worse. Difference is not a value. It's an observation, a context.
- Treat your running body as you would a child – be gentle, fair and understanding, but firm. Don't put up with any nonsense.
- Keep going forwards. Progress is unstoppable and every step is an achievement.
- Run longer and faster only when your body makes it clear that it's ready. Give it a nudge once in a while, on one of the good days, just to see what happens, in case it's being coy.
- Use a watch only to tell you when it's time to go home.

Train your mind and, in time, your body will follow wherever you want to go. Soon enough you won't notice that the road ahead is all uphill. Or if you do, you won't care anymore.

Quantum Running

For a long time you might think you've made no progress – but you have. You just can't recognise it yet, and until you can, your brain won't let you use it.

Fundamental particles, so the theory goes, exist only in specific states, and nowhere in between. When changing energy levels (as it apparently likes to do), a particle will vanish from one level and, exactly no time later, appear at another, without leaving any observable trace of how it got there. In the same instant it's here, not here and somewhere else.

Running does something very similar. In the early stages, physical adaptation appears to happen in steps rather than as a regular linear progression. After a period of no obvious progress there's an unannounced 'Oh wow!' moment.

There may in fact have been a continuous physical adaptation leading to that jump, but in the absence of observation, as with Schrödinger's boxed cat, its state is indeterminate – it might be there, or it might not.

The brain is conservative – it doesn't gamble, leaving it open to uncertainty to make a staircase out of a slope.

Body Language

Motivation does not like surprises. It's easier to commit when you have a good idea of what's going on.

Patience will be rewarded. Soon enough, experience will teach you the subtle grammar in the regular aches, the tight muscles and the tidal ebb and flow of energy. You will discover that your brain is over-protective of your body, and that the tiredness vanishes as you run, the pains dissolve as you warm up, the heaviness is just a test of determination, the restraints of gravity and friction are illusions. Your body will start to talk for itself, bursting to tell you of its adaptations, and you will be amazed at what you can do.

One thing your new body won't ever tell you to do is to stop.

There will be days when you wonder whose body you're in – this one seems so different. You will see yourself as someone else.

Like Scheherazade's endless magical tales, your body will now tease you. It will leave you hungry, wanting more. It will tempt you to challenge yourself, to hurdle the shadows in your head. By now, these are games you like to play. More often than not the hurdles evaporate before you get to them.

More and more things seem possible.

You keep going.

You are There

We each climb a different mountain, but at the top we're all the same distance from wherever it was we started.

Every mountain has a peak. Above is empty space. As a racer you might have gone higher, but you wouldn't survive for long. We were not made to be stars, to sparkle in the void. As a runner, ice cream eater and human this is it, the sustainable limit of necessity.

Your feet have carried you safely home.

You'll know you've arrived when you stop asking how high you can go. The question hasn't been answered: it's just ceased to be important. The transformation is complete. There's no going back. There's nowhere to go back to. Your past now belongs to someone else.

Look around, at where you started, and far into the distance. Enjoy the view. From here, everything is beautiful. All this life is yours.

Your willpower and ability are now the same – you can go anywhere you want. There's no longer any need to dream. You are free to live.

It's time for an ice cream, the waffle cone, like a mirror lake, faithfully reflecting the perfect triangle of your personal mountain and the angle of your ascent.

Elysium

Homo Sapiens has done great things. To be fair, though, he's also done some fairly questionable things. Wisdom is not bound by morality. History is full of well-read sociopaths, erudite despots and evil geniuses.

The greatest of the Homeric heroes, Achilles, demi-god and all round legend, embodied flawless honour, faith and prowess. It's hardly a co-incidence that he was also revered as 'the great runner'.

The union of gods and humans might be less common today than at the time of Troy, but running and ice cream can overcome any deficiencies of parentage. Born of mortal sweat and frozen desserts, our actions, like those of Achilles, will be inspired by angels.

This is *Homo Sapiens sp. Glacialis Currens* – 'smart running man full of ice (cream)'.

Look in the mirror. What do you see? What species are you? What species do you want to be?

You have a choice.

Advanced soles

Travelling by foot

Body

Fashion is a trap – the graceless child of competition and deceit. Resist its seductive call. Simplicity works better.

Stretching

For some it's a religion. I don't believe in their gods. The shortening and stiffness of muscles feels like a natural adaptation for running. Spring theory also suggests a better transfer of rebound energy through less flexible legs. That makes sense to me. I will never again touch my toes.

Carbo-Loading

A normal diet will supply enough energy for an average run. And if you run low, let your muscles eat fat. You're carrying it with you anyhow and everyone can spare a bit, so you may as well burn it.

Fuel on the run

Only on long runs. When it's needed, I *eat* energy rather than *drink* it. Like a car, I keep fuel and water separate. This might be a little idiosyncratic, but I believe it works better. It seems to me to be how the body was designed.

Re-fuel

It's a fairly basic energy equation. For each hour of running you need about 800 Calories – that's 700 for the exercise and 100 for your elevated post-exercise metabolic rate.

Supplements

Unless you chance upon a treasure map or a genii, there's nothing that comes in a bottle that will do much for your long term enjoyment of running.

iPods

This is not the rhythm you are looking for. Listen to yourself run, and the world around you. Batteries are not required.

Shoes

It shouldn't be a question of shoes or no shoes, but what type of shoes. There are shoes that simulate barefoot and shoes that don't. Take your pick. I wouldn't leave home without protection. I want to run every day - and there are rocks, glass, thorns and modern surfaces out there with other ideas. I like shoes.

Cross Training

For the days when you can't run - if there are any. I have no experience of cross training.

Breathing

A focus on correct breathing can be a good alternative to self-pity when things get difficult – slow in, fast out; use your diaphragm (draw 'navel to spine' when you exhale); and stand tall as you run.

Time

Run as often as you can. Occasionally try to run for longer. Sometimes, when you feel good, try to run faster. The great thing about trying is seeing just how often you not only do what you set out to do, but do more.

Interest

Think like a tourist. Entertain your senses; go on a journey; or play. Stay off the road whenever possible. Enjoy the passing landscapes and the daily differences of light, colour and sound. There's no excuse for a boring run.

Rest

Ease back into it after an extended break, even if you feel great. Cardio fitness and bio-mechanics degrade at different rates. It's best to keep them in synch to avoid injury.

Soul

I believe…

I'm justified in saying 'up yours' to time, inertia and gravity.

I can see the passage of time in the mirror, but I don't feel it. The dry, grey brush of autumn may have painted my chin, but it hasn't touched my soul. The future still looks big and full - and green, an eternity of spring.

I have a partial exemption from most of the seven deadly sins, most of the time.

Running every day isn't training. It's part of waking up and re-assembling the senses.

The feeling of dread at the start of a run is just the departure of dreams. It won't last.

In the early morning I can run with kangaroos, who don't remember to be afraid of people until after breakfast.

In the privacy of dawn I can play aeroplanes, arms spread like wings, without having to pretend I was airing my armpits or stretching.

The rhythm of breathing makes it easy to think about one thing at a time, uninterrupted.

No problem has been properly considered until I've taken it for a run.

Something that once seemed difficult is now natural.

If it gets tough, it only gets so tough and no more – and from then on it doesn't seem so bad.

There's a good reason for the bad days – and whatever it is, it's not that I've suddenly 'lost it'. The running body doesn't work that way. These days build character.

There comes a moment in almost every run where I feel more energetic, more positive and more at peace with the world than at any other time in the day.

Running doesn't waste energy on worry, frustration or anger.

It's normal to finish a solid run feeling better than I did at the start.

Most runs end up lasting longer than I'd planned – not because I was going slowly, but because I wanted more and wasn't ready to go home.

Distance is not a challenge: it's an opportunity.

I am not ruled by a compass. There are no pre-determined directions. The only fixed point is home, and no matter which way I go, that's where I end up.

The only drug I need is the sound of my shoes on gravel.

Running is not an addiction. It's indivisible from me. I breathe. I run. I am. Three sides of the same coin.

Running in the rain, splashing in puddles washes off the years.

Time is not absolute. Real time is not measured in hours, minutes and seconds, but in moments. The more you run, the more moments you get.

I can experience adventures most people could not imagine.

My most vivid and powerful experiences are not dreams. I live with my eyes open.

I can eat all the ice cream I want.

I run just because. Not running is something other people do.

…and I never start out thinking that any day will be my last and that I should live it exceptionally, but if I did, I'd still go for a run. I'm leaving feet first.

Water Hazard

The study of sweat may not be appealing, but a runner's loss of water and electrolytes is the source of an interesting debate.

There are some who say that runners should drink before they feel thirsty, should drink to replace sweat loss (weight), and should replace electrolytes. Some of these people may also offer to sell you sport drinks.

Others argue that moderate dehydration is OK, that thirst is a better indicator of need, and that sweat is less salty than normal body fluids - so the concentration of electrolytes in the body actually increases.

Whatever you do, you can't avoid supporting one side or the other.

I never drink on a run less than 2 hours (unless in extreme conditions), so I'll inevitably lose weight while running. When I need to drink, I drink plain water and take a solid electrolyte replacement. This works for me. In either case, there's nothing quite like the joy of re-hydration after a good run!

Warning: Dehydration is not the greatest risk. Drinking a lot of water during strenuous exercise <u>without</u> electrolyte supplementation is potentially much more dangerous. I wouldn't do it.

Footprints

Happiness is a function of how much we take - and what we leave behind.

Occupy the Garden.

The Greek philosopher Epicurus has suffered more than his fair share of injustice before the court of history. He's been reviled and misrepresented by generations of otherwise respectable bigots who rail with an intemperate passion against works that they seem not to have read or understood. If Epicurus is remembered at all today, more often than not it's only in the word 'epicurean', a derisive word which has as little relationship to his teachings as an iPhone has to an apple tree.

This is the price Epicurus paid for doubting the concern of the ancient gods for humanity's successes and failures. Divine punishment and reward, according to Epicurus, are not to be found in the afterlife – principally because there isn't one. Nor are they found in this life, as the immortal gods are busy with their own affairs and really aren't all that interested in what we're doing. We are, he taught, completely responsible for own destiny and the results of our actions.

Epicurus certainly knew how to pick a fight. If his view that humans were simply atoms animated by a mortal soul wasn't enough to offend nearly every known speculative orthodoxy, his insistence on personal responsibility annoyed just about everyone. Generally, people would prefer to have someone (or something) else to blame when things don't go according to their own flawed plans.

Already off to a bad start as an alleged heretic, Epicurus has also been condemned as a profligate hedonist. If there is no eternity and no judgement, he argued, then this life is all we've got, and we might as well do whatever we can to be happy until our atoms are recycled. It's easy to see how this might be misinterpreted as some form of insouciant, ethically questionable, *dolce vita* manifesto - but that's only if you completely ignore the essential teaching that the happiness we seek is to be found exclusively in restrained self-sufficiency and the rejection of excess. The greatest happiness, according to Epicurus, comes from having the least needs.

That position also was clearly not going to be popular with a great many people who felt that collecting things (usually money, power and other people's misery or fear) was important.

Fortunately, bad theory doesn't absolutely preclude good results. No matter how you feel about Epicurus' theology, his conclusions on the visible world can stand alone and deserve to be taken seriously. The world may be a place of infinite subtlety, but in every respect that matters, it has not changed much since the days when Epicurus tried to make sense of it, surrounded by friends in The Garden - his school outside Athens.

As Buckminster Fuller's 'spaceship earth' hurtles around the sun, its environmental systems choked, the crewmembers morally disabled, deluded and deceived, communications channels silenced by noise, the superstructure dented and its fuel running low, Epicurus' doctrine of individual responsibility and the need for simplicity, may be more relevant today than it ever was. Something has to give – and that should be us.

Reducing our own demands and offering a hand of fairness would be a good start. It's within our ability to do this much, to commit, to take personal responsibility, to be realistic about our needs and wants, to be gentle and kind, to be optimistic and confident – an honest friend to ourselves, to each other and to this fragile blue ball, the only place in the known universe where we can live.

If that sounds rather familiar, it should. It's exactly the same way we learned to run. It's what ice cream has shown us is right.

We've done it before. We can do it again. We can save the world the same way we saved ourselves. With a smile.

The Big Bang

The sensation of happiness is not the event itself. Instead, it's a gift from a second ago, the sweetly narcotic afterglow of a singularity, the echo of a lost moment of disembodied *wantlessness* that passed unnoticed and unreachable beneath the threshold of the senses. For a while afterwards, in the lengthening shadows of decaying optimism, the sharp edges of all our cares, needs and unfulfilled goals are softer than usual. And we smile.

When at last night falls, when fear's jagged, slathering monsters and the ghosts of ghosts have come back to haunt us, we long for a return of the light.

The question is: do I wait for these silent moments to occur by accident, or do I try to put myself in a position where I'm more likely than not to run into one?

I choose the second, more favourable alternative. I'll run. And then I'll eat ice cream.

It's my future. Let there be light.

Click.

Outrageous Adventures

Going places, seeing things, getting lost and slaying dragons

Marathon Des Sables

The Marathon des Sables, a 250km race through the South Moroccan Sahara Desert, has acquired an almost legendary status. The Tour de France of desert footraces, MdS claims to be the 'toughest running race in the world'. Everyone knows this isn't true, but such is the respect for the event that no-one argues too much. It's tough enough.

Preparing for MdS is a process of distillation. The rules require you to carry in your backpack all the food and gear you will need for the 7 days of the event – except a tent and water (which are graciously provided by the organisers). So, you start with what you want, and then take only what you can't live without (and are prepared to carry). That shouldn't amount to much. Survival doesn't require a great deal: comfort, only a little more. You should be honest - and brutal - with your weaknesses and idiosyncrasies to reduce the risk of excess. Even then, a large and experienced team of doctors, aid station marshals and assorted race crew is on hand at all points of the course to cover your more egregious mistakes, or, if everything goes wrong, to respond rapidly to your distress rocket.

The camps at the start and end of each stage are small, mobile cities, temporary oases, decked with flags, buzzing with wireless communications, excitement, news crews and the constant to and fro of people and vehicles, either returned from the course or not yet started. The participants' tents are two sided Berber sails, black drapes which flap and wobble in the wind. Veils of sand rain through the loosely stitched material. If you lie on your back you can see the sky. Campsites are almost always hard, dry, ancient lake beds (the only places where tent pegs can actually do anything). The thin rugs on the floor of the tents would probably be advertised anywhere else as 'ethnic and charming': here they hold down the sand, but do little to soften the rocks.

These shade shelters define a communal space for 8 increasingly ragged guests. You soon learn to live with the fine powder that coats your teeth and eyelids, with the dry latrines that hide nothing, and with the unconscious bodily indiscretions of your tent mates. In the desert, the first things to go are taste and modesty, replaced with a new order of manners. The desert doesn't care, and smiles or frowns for its own amusement. You just get on with it. You try to laugh at the indignities and the incongruity of words like 'dainty' and 'precious' that belong to less authentic places. After all, you chose to be here, and it's only for a week. Almost anything should be tolerable for that length of time.

Air temperature water is distributed at each camp and check point in 1.5L plastic bottles – every bottle and lid is marked with your race number, and you're responsible, under threat of public humiliation and disqualification, for their proper disposal. A single misplaced lid could ruin your day. Little things are important. The desert is to be left as it was found, a place of startling contradictions, a meeting point of the living and the dead, where black scarabs scrawl signatures in the moving sand under the midday sun.

Each participant has a strict water ration which must cover re-hydration, cooking and, if any is left, washing socks. It's not really worth wasting water trying to wash yourself – you'll be dirty as soon as you're clean and, in any case, the caked dust is the best sun protection.

The water bottles can be cut down to make a useful cup, saving the weight of carrying your own. With temperatures reaching 55C, meals can be re-heated by the sun in this makeshift cookware. A ziplock bag and a small square of black plastic make a good thermal collector that also protects against the dust. A medium sized rock on the corner stops your dinner blowing away.

Night falls fast in the desert. The flat twilight colours only last briefly, as do those moments when you want to walk barefoot, treading lightly in the cooling sand between long camel bush thorns and translucent scorpions. The sky becomes huge. Some people stay up, trading fabulous lies in LED pools. Others lie in wait for sleep, saving their batteries. With the hard ground, the wind, the aches and the aura of strangeness, sleep is elusive – there's lots of horizontal, but little unconsciousness. If sleep comes, it's short-lived. 'Yallah!' – the rousing cry of the blue coated Berbers demanding their tents. The entire encampment is broken down each day and moved on, starting in the icy pre-dawn light. It always seems to be your tent that gets taken first. There is no mercy, no delay. It's time to go.

Events like MdS leave have no respect for reputations earned elsewhere. Success in single day events or road races of any distance is a poor guide to how you will fare day after day in the heat, cold and unpredictability of the desert. Every year, world class athletes are forced to face their weaknesses, and it's not just a case of bad luck. It's clear that there is something happening that can't be measured on conventional scales. It's acceptance. Talent is an asset, no doubt, as is preparation, but in addition to any other specific adaptation, you need to listen and submit. You cannot be indifferent or proud and expect to be well received.

As the temperature climbs with the helicopters and camera drones in the cloudless sky, the next stage unrolls beyond the music powered bravado of the start line and the bright circle of sponsors' banners. The course, slightly different each year, takes you through a succession of seemingly empty places with names – like Oued Ziz, its baked mud a warped monochrome mosaic of peeling, fractal cracks; the impossibly perfect, wind carved dunes of Erg Znaïgui; the twin plateaus imposing either side of the oasis of El Maharch; and the towering ramparts of Jebel Oftal, standing between the wide, rock-strewn plains of Oued Rehris and the setting sun. These are empty places, but not dead. Their names are a sign of life, the heartbeat of people without maps, the inheritance of the smiling, lilting children who appear, often on broken bicycles, at points along the course, envious of the pitiful luxuries in your backpack, at home in the sand in their sand coloured homes. We are not the trail blazing explorers some competitors might like to believe. We are guests.

The finish line is a catalogue of emotions – there are some in awe of their own achievement, cheering and yelling to anyone who will listen; some relieved it's over, at last free to waste water on tears; and still others, perhaps battered and broken, disappointed that their race did not go as planned. Then there are those people, smiling quietly or even blank, who are not sure what just happened, but know that they are not yet ready to return to their previous reality. For years to come, haunted by a sense of terrible beauty, they will try to see into that blank spot in their memory where they were something more than they thought possible.

There are debts due and payable to the desert. MdS brings many good things to the people of the Sahara, among them solar-powered clean water wells, schools and community development centres, but all these are little more than fair rent for the use of their backyard.

There's nothing heroic about the race. This is not *terra incognita*. The course is well marked and the roadbook shows the way with elegant diagrams and detailed instructions. There are no explorers here: getting lost is difficult. You're never out of touch – every evening between and 5 and 6 o'clock, e-mail messages from family, friends, supporters and sometimes inspired strangers are printed out and delivered to your tent; so too, the communications tent allows you to send e-mail and make satellite phone calls to anywhere on earth where someone cares about you. Every contingency, even flood, has been carefully anticipated and managed. No-one's here against their will. The organisers have kept no secrets - everyone has come to the desert with eyes wide open. It's a great, magnificent, even spiritual experience, but it's also selfish and self-indulgent. To pay for this privilege, the least anyone can do is to go home a better person, with a well-defined sense of insignificance and an indomitable will to give a damn about a whole lot of things that previously seemed unimportant or too far away. All debts to the Sahara will then be considered settled.

The rust coloured water will soon run clear under a warm shower when you return to the land of ice creams, but the sand stays in your soul. No-one who has been there ever really leaves. The Sahara, the perfect balance of fear and beauty, is an indelible puzzle.

It's insoluble.

The TRACK Outback Ultramarathon

Like most monsters, The TRACK was a magnetic hybrid of mixed parentage. On one side was the same French sense of the theatre of the absurd that gave birth to the Marathon des Sables. On the other, from Australia's undead heart, came the set design, the open horizons and emptiness of the never-never. In May 2011, a cast of 23 runners representing 10 countries played out this unique drama, making up the script as they went, starting and finishing far from every modern somewhere.

The course was the longest ever in the world of multi-day races, stretching 520km from a start in the deceptive serenity of Ellery Creek in the West McDonnell Ranges. From there it tracked west through the long, scooped valleys full of hypodermic spinifex and the smashed dolomite ridge lines of the Larapinta Trail to Glen Helen Gorge; and then further west, south and finally east along overgrown bush trails to the community of Hermannsberg. Continuing south, the course followed an ancient aboriginal trade route through the Palaeozoic meanders of the Finke River Gorges to the dry cattle country of Angas Downs and Curtin Springs, with its abundance of corrugations, laterite and salt. Finally there was a right turn at the mesa of Mt. Connor, before a character-building 135km stage into the sunset and night in search of Australia's spiritual heart at the end of Lasseter Highway: Uluru, rising from the strange land of the desert oaks.

For nine days we ran until we walked, and then we ran some more, until that was all we could do. We ran, we lived and we became the flowing blood in the narrow, dry, red dirt veins of the outback. And, as if revived by our flow, the desert awoke from the dreamtime and told us its stories.

At the start, it's not uncommon to see other participants as dishearteningly younger, stronger, fitter and better prepared for the challenge. Even if this first impression is right, it's rarely a good indication of how they will manage what is about to take place. Soon you find out that it's a game of chance, that no-one really knows for sure how to get ready physically for an event of this scale, and that it's what you can't see that will really count once the race kicks off. When the sun stalks directly overhead and the hawks watch from their high circles, when the direction is vague and the end seems as far away as the start, the ability to deal with doubt will be at least as important as physical fitness.

I lined up for The TRACK with an uncomfortable feeling that I might be out of my depth, that I might not even have the right to hope to finish. All I had was a powerful sense of longing. For what?

This race was twice the length of any multi-stage event I'd done before. With an average day of 60kms on tough terrain, icy nights in plastic tents dripping with condensation, the irresistible onslaught of a mouse plague rippling under, over and through the camp, suicide squads of flies, blood, infection, no reasonable prospect of ice cream, sand and still more damned red, slippery, deep sand, the end soon looked to be receding, slithering after the King Brown that crossed my path and vanished into the untracked scrub. For a while, I was not sure I was sad to see either go.

It's in the nature of moments like this that you end up doing things you can't believe, let alone explain - and so it happened. This is where you learn a lot about yourself, about how much you don't know, and about how the more you know, the less your knowledge represents of all there is to know. The truth is that the things you can explain don't add up to very much. Everything else is just daylight magic.

So, you ignore your doubts, fall into your natural rhythm, breathe, count, listen, manage resources, look for signs, calculate, hum, laugh, grit your teeth, sigh, breathe some more and let wonder lead you through the rising tide of sameness to places you've never been before. As much as anything, this is what running is about – acceptance, both of the things you think you know and of those you definitely don't. Running makes the most sense when you don't think about it too much. It has its own uncertainty principle: you can rationalise running or you can run – but you can't do both at the same time. That's as exciting as it is liberating.

You press on because you can't go back and you run because that's who you are. For now, it's all you are. Whatever you might be elsewhere isn't here, doesn't mean anything and can't help.

And then, not suddenly, maybe not even quite soon enough, but inevitably, there was Uluru, unmoved, pale, silent and wise under a full moon at the stroke of midnight, standing behind the finishing banner. This was the end of The TRACK – the end of adrenaline and the start of pain, a flood in a dry place

The galleries of memory will display the images of this colourful band of adventurers in the back of beyond – spread out along barely visible trails, a slowly stretching snake under a big sky; silhouetted against the sunrise in the golden dust on Ernst Giles Rd; sitting in the shade of a Red River Gum near Illamurta, waiting for the water to boil in an assortment of ultra-light cooking pots; a silent huddle, shaking off sleep around a crackling fire in the darkness at Serpentine Gorge; dazed and hopeful, lining up for water at a check point on course; or wandering past the broken fences and rusted remains of historical optimism. Somewhere also there are the results, laid out in tables of names and numbers with national flags.

These are the facts, vivid and memorable, but less than the real story - a superficial report in history's late evening news. The truth of The TRACK is not something that can be captured in an instant, quantified, or reduced to a narrative laid out in neat, grammatical paragraphs. There's a dark place in the brain that stores sensations, complete, unedited and individual, and doesn't look for connections or significance. The real events of The TRACK are safe in that wordless part of my head, where the entire experience can be re-lived in a single moment, in a shiver that I can't share and a slight, adjectival smile that is most often mistaken for something else.

On reflection, this is what that sense of longing I'd felt on the start line was all about – for an experience that would leave me staggering and speechless. The long days and isolation of The TRACK became the last stage in a journey that began years before, a running odyssey that closely shadowed Dante through the nine circles of training Hell and the revelations on Purgatory's mountain of adaptation, all the way to the dictionary transcending Empyrean.

Some days you do actually get what you want. After that, nothing is quite the same again. The longing lies close to the surface, like a shadow in the sea. It's unsettling, but mostly in a good way – a dolphin, not a shark.

It does make you wonder, though. There's no going back, but is there more?

Any Day, Almost Anywhere

In the park nearby there are kilometres of mountain bike trails. Early in the morning, when the bikers are still riding in their sleep, dreaming of soft tails and cranks, this playground of jumps, banked turns, tree-lined single track and unseen things that rustle in the dry scrub is all mine.

Each day I run for 60 – 90 minutes, sometimes longer, rarely less. That's somewhere over 6,000 kilometres per year for no reason that would generally be accepted as good. I start in the dark, or with the first hints of light, and often I'm home before anyone is awake. In these margins of the days, I meet my other self, the person I call me, but who now feels like someone else, somehow bio-mechanically upgraded. I admire his abilities and achievements in a way that I couldn't do if they were only mine. Together we conquer the fortresses of the imagination, chasing rain drops, brushing aside the leaf-gloved fingers of beckoning trees, sliding into gravel corners, wrestling free from the webs of giant spiders and hurdling piles of rocks and logs full of treachery and tangles. The sights and smells of the bush fire us on to victory. When it's time to leave, our flag flies proudly from the highest peaks. This place is ours. Tomorrow and every day after that, glistening like heroes, as excited as kids, unstoppable, we will take it back again.

When I don't go to the bush trails, I turn to the coast. The beach at dawn is rarely ever in between. It is either mirror calm, or tormented by sandy gales. On the quiet days I leave the first footsteps on the flat sand below last night's high tide, joining the dots of the starfish at the water's edge. I watch my shadow emerge as the sun reaches out from the sea, our feet coming together and parting like the waves and the shore. I meet the glazed party goers struggling home, shoes in hand; the insomniac, still life photographers bargaining silently with the sun and clouds for the perfect light; and the silent fishermen, standing entranced, willing fish onto their baited hooks while waiting patiently until it's no longer too early for a beer. Also there are the dawn dog walkers, hoping, with sideways glances, to empty out their hounds before having to deal with the mess at home. And the frowning, busy business people, connected invisibly to later time zones, oblivious to the miracles of sunrise as they follow their worries, sleepwalking through the shallows and into the next big deal. It's a world caught between amazement and bemusement.

On the wild days, there are fewer games to play. I'm left alone, seemingly always facing the wrong way in the biting howl of a wind tunnel. I just laugh at how silly it all is, and lean into the wind. Eventually it's over and once again, I didn't quite lose.

These everyday adventures may be subtle, but they're no less real than a desert crossing or a night under the open skies of nowhere. It makes me wonder sometimes – should I tell those who aren't there, or do I keep them for me? I guess, in the end, the important parts of space and time are flexible. All I need to do is run, and my imagination opens doors to secret kingdoms without clocks, where there's always another dragon to slay.

Late

Running: it was never really about learning – but about remembering.

Then

When you're young, ageing seems optional. It's something that only happens to old people. The future is far, far away. Just like Pluto, there's no need to plan to go there yet.

Then one day, for no obvious reason, you wake up to the pounding of the biological clock. The mortality train has arrived at your station, whistling and steaming, with its cargo of cares. As you rattle along towards an unknown destination, out the window the world has lost its infinity. Forever has vanished – seconds have numbers and days can be counted. Peter Pan lied. Never Never Land never ever was.

Oh dear. That was unexpected.

Time will tick away mercilessly, but decay and submission can be deferred. Running and eating ice cream, their roots entangled in our younger days, drawing deep from the well of memories, combine to produce fairy dust. Growing up is a process of forgetting what's natural and good, and of losing faith in our own ability and imagination. When we run, we do what a child does and we see the world through more innocent eyes. It's not a perfect fountain of youth, but it's more than any alchemist ever achieved - and about as good as it gets. At least in action and outlook we are young again. For a while the wretched ticking clock is quiet.

Inevitably, however, time will demand adjustments. Then, more than ever, it is important to stick to your own rhythm, to maintain a constant perception of effort, and to ignore those photogenic outliers – statistical anomalies who run against the trend. They're no more a benchmark now than they were before, and there's little to be learned from their training schedules and achievements. They are a rare species, human maybe, but not from the same brand of DNA. They are born to run fast, far or both, for longer, and have no more of an idea why that is so than why it is not for everyone else. It doesn't make them better or happier. They just are - as are we all.

Later

Instinct suggests that one day it should be time to stop. Or to try to stop. But it's a capitalist world, and there's a fare to be paid for the ride you've enjoyed. Fitness is like any other commodity - if you can't get more, then you still want to protect what you've got. It's going to be hard to let go. Also, the runner's heart is different – it's big, slow and full of passion. Can it forget? Can it live less? Stopping will require some careful planning.

Running - it's not starting that is the real problem, or even continuing, it's stopping. Maybe that's running's final gift – to run through life's last winter into the sunset, to greet whatever is next as though it were a favourite ice cream and the long, fun-filled summer days of your childhood. Go in peace.

Until then – 'Rage, rage against the dying of the light.'

'*Do Not Go Gentle Into That Good* Night' - Dylan Thomas

Next

My journeys through nowhere, real and imagined, have convinced me that whatever the powers of design or chance that rule the universe, there are no plans for our complete annihilation. Even nowhere I've found no nothingness. It's teeming with *beyondness* – beyond comprehension and calculation, even beyond imagination. Life curves away from us, like the surface of the earth, and another somewhere, different but not completely, sits tantalisingly just over the horizon of our senses. And perhaps more beyond that.

It's the same as all those places in the 'empty' Sahara, where nowhere and somewhere are identical, separated only by perspective. Or those unseen adaptations on the way up the hill – present, but invisible because we didn't know what we were looking for until we had passed it. Or the strange behaviour of sub-atomic particles, which are in all possible states at once - until we look at them. That's the human condition, to live in a world bounded by imperfect vision. No matter what our vantage point, we cannot see all of it at once - nor any of it from all possible angles.

Most days, for a moment in the middle of a run on some trail, or on some beach in the still twilight of dawn, when nothing else matters, I get that same shiver that started after The TRACK, the sense of a wider horizon, and an invitation from life – not my life, but all possible life – to experience things I can't see or describe. Big things.

I'm not ready yet, but there will come a time when I am.

There's that same sequence once again: a hint of something more, a promise, a 'here' and a 'there', and a remarkable transformation on the road from one to the other. This looks a lot like another journey up another mountain. And another homecoming.

I've had a practice run – surely it can only get easier. I'd better pack my shoes…

In the end, there's no end: just the continuity of change and new, outrageous adventures that we can't yet imagine. Here we go again…

6am Tuesday (Part 2)

Exactly a week ago I saved a life. Today I lost one.

On a morning tinged with grace, my run stopped where Tuesday's child lay in a circle of trees, injured and scared. We just looked at each other. Helpless. Both of us. All of us. There was no happy ending, no miracle. On a calm, clear day, like on any other day, we were all just so totally useless. Broken kangaroos can't be repaired.

For the dreamers at home in bed, anaesthetised, the gunshot probably sounded like another *Hardenbergia Comptoniana* seed pod bursting on a warm summer morning amid the cheers of a choir of cicadas, launching a new life. In the moment of silence that followed, a reluctant tide of dark blood spread over the cushion of dry leaves and soaked into the soil.

So, running takes you to the naked edge, to where fortune could go either way, to where nothing is more valuable, more fragile, more beautiful than life. Even through tears of frustration, that's a good place to be.

About the Author

Andrew is one of Australia's most accomplished multi-day desert racers. He has competed in the Marathon des Sables 3 times, in the process, in 2007, becoming the highest placed Australian in the 22 year history of the event (up to that point), and then winning the veterans division in 2008. In 2010 he was second in the inaugural Australian Outback Marathon, and in 2011 he finished third overall in the world's longest multi-stage race, The TRACK Outback Ultramarathon, in central Australia. He runs every day and regularly organises charity running events, including, in 2010, 'The Longest Day' the first ever single day run from Cape Leeuwin to Cape Naturaliste (135km) in SW Western Australia.

Andrew lives in Dunsborough, Western Australia, with his family and 2 Abyssinian cats called Henry who tolerate with great kindness his attempt to play the banjo.

www.ingramcontent.com/pod-product-compliance
Lightning Source LLC
Chambersburg PA
CBHW081228040426
42445CB00016B/1914